Lady With Unicorn Tapestry

Lady With Unicorn Tapestry

Poems by

Paul Francis Malamud

Cover design by Shay Culligan

ISBN: 978-1-952326-81-3

Kelsay Books
502 South 1040 East, A-119
American Fork, Utah, 84003

To family and friends

Acknowledgments

A number of poems in this volume made their first appearance in the following periodicals and anthologies: *Blue Unicorn, Edge City Review, The Lyric, Troubadour 2000, Trinacria, Think Magazine, of Western Colorado State University.* My thanks to the editors.

Some of these appeared in an earlier collection of the author's verse, titled *Old Poems, New Translations.*

Contents

Book VI

Book I

Italy, 1956

The old monk may have been surprised to see
a Jewish man in a brown overcoat
touring the Giotto frescoes, in Assisi
only ten years after the War—his son
pallid and timid—but he cheerfully
took our picture with Dad's borrowed Leica,
me huddling against Dad's overcoat.
Then Dad and I went out on to the terrace
where St. Francis had spoken to the birds.
Dad was delighted, awestruck—I was bored.
I'm awestruck now to think that I was bored,
but I missed Donald Duck comic books and Coke.

In the mornings, Dad walked me to the school bus,
through the smoky pastels of winter Rome,
and then at night, he'd come to meet the bus.
If I'd done my fourth-grade math, I might get a comic,
or roast chestnuts from the chestnut man,
hot off the smoking charcoal, wrapped in foil.
I ate two: Dad demanded one, a tribute.
"My father didn't have much of a life," he'd say,
"and our relationship wasn't always good,
but later in life you'll remember this."
And yes, he made it real, because to him
it was real—had to be—after that War.

"The golds, the tans, the pinks, the yellows, grays,
so different from America—so rich,"
Mom and Dad would say after a walk—
like happy birds, sometimes unhappy ones—
both in their early forties, a better life
starting after poverty and war.

We visited the Spanish steps
at Easter, the steps covered with carnations.
I still remember carnations and the heat,
how they asked a man to take their picture
sitting together on the Spanish steps,
hands twined, bemused, and smiling in the sun.

Weekends I'd walk with Mom long distances
to small stores, some with the rich leather smells,
or cheese smells, and pizzas behind glass,
and the ultimate pleasure, an éclair;
and in the summer, as a family, through
piazzas—fountains, Tritons, Nereids,
twisting dolphins leaping free of marble,
silvery water chattering at the sky.

Yes, it's true, and I remember him
just now in the way he said I would—
as my father, an affectionate Jew—
waiting for me where the school bus had stopped
to put his arm on my shoulder then,
and take me back home in the Roman dusk,
walking happily in his rumpled tweed jacket
past the elevator cage and up scuffed stairs
into the lit apartment, as I ran.

Catacombs

What fun it was in 1956
to walk with parents through the catacombs
of ancient Rome, so dark and underground.
The unctuous guides were used to giving thrills
to American tourists, popular, then,
"benevolent" victors. Fired torches flared
as we walked through tunnels with recesses
in the stone walls—now open—bits of bone
left by medieval tomb robbers—or sealed,
with marble slabs that still had ancient Latin
carved upon them—names of Christian martyrs—
buried in secret, in the ancient world,
where Roman legions couldn't touch the bones.
And afterwards, when we came up to light
Mom and Dad laughed—I brushed my Madras shirt.
I'd thought maybe it would be scary—but the gold-
red flaring of the torches, blood on stone,
kept me entranced. Back in the bright sun,
in the enchanted Mediterranean heat
of a dry June in sunny Italy,
it was clear how much nicer it was to be
an American boy in 1956
than a dead Roman. After that, I'm sure
I asked for an orange soda and gelato,
my parents, laughing, chattering with friends,
as we got into a cramped tinny postwar car.
I watched in wonder as the driver shifted the gear,
and the car lurched forward, going to more fun:
maybe a comic book or puppet show.

Pompeii, 1957

It was about heat and smells, the smell of dry
sun on dry land, ancient earth, brick, stone
the air that smelled so burnt, the scented brush,
and marble, in a froth of grass and trees.
I wanted orange soda, and an ice
in a paper cone, but knew the wish was hopeless—
"No, you'll spoil dinner." I didn't ask
because I knew what Mom would say, and Dad
wouldn't resist her, in her realm of food.
So this was it, Pompeii—I ran around
cavorting in the ruins, half-amused
to hear the guide, then leave the group, to stare
at some old pillar, or dim paintings in
a shadowed room. The museum had
the famous casts, explained so carefully,
of the dead Romans, covered up by ash,
the hollow empty body shapes filled up
with liquid plaster, through small earthen holes,
revealing—who had lived, and how they died.
We went into the first room. They were white.
I stared. "Look at the detail on the clothes,"
Dad whispered; Mom agreed. After a while
they looked at me and said that they were going
into another room, but to stay there.
I walked around and stared some more, until
they both came out, Mom talking, slightly fast,
"Oh, that poor boy—that child—oh my dear."
"Honey," he said, exasperated, "that's
from two thousand years ago, two thousand, and
there's no more horror in it, it's just a
plaster cast, that's all it is. We're here."
I gathered they'd seen something very bad
in the far room, and asked if I might go.

Dad hesitated—looked at Mom. "Well, maybe,
if you really want to, but there are
some mildly disturbing casts there, and that's why
they have the sign there by the door. And so, maybe,
you should wait a few years, until you're older,
then you can go into the other room.
There are some things there that are—difficult."
Curious, I soon bounced outdoors
into the swift oasis of the sunset,
praying for an evening of spaghetti,
yet wondering what happened to that boy;
any uneasiness about his fate
was soon washed out by the cool garden joy.
You know, that trip to Pompeii was my last:
I'll never know exactly what they saw.

She-Wolf

Poor Mom, she was so warm and loving,
yet she had this wolfish temperament,
and could reduce me to tears, when I was a kid.
She was so angry and high strung sometimes.
When we went to Italy in '56,
I absolutely fell in love in fourth grade
with the story of Romulus and Remus raised
by a she-wolf. Mom liked the way I talked
about it, saw me looking through shop
windows at marble she-wolves, little ones
sold then to tourists. Finally, sometime after
I had had German measles, she bought me
a small bronze she-wolf suckling the twins,
and later gave me a small marble one.
"Do you like the Roman wolf?" she said, and laughed.
"Look how strong she is, and how she's guarding
both the little boys, with that fierce face."

Bedtime, Fifth Grade, Oregon

The moment I'd gone upstairs, Dad turned on
the Zenith radio. I knew he was there,
downstairs, rubbing his worn slippers together,
settling, relaxed, into the Danish chair

to read a book, and correct student papers.
The theme from Handel's *Water Music* pealed
at 9 PM, the classical music hour.
Each in his way, our happiness was sealed:

happy me, with a warm, loving, father
guarding the house of which I felt so fond;
happy him, gold-leafed harmonies, baroque,
wafting him to great Europe, the beyond.

Generator Light, 1958

One day my father bought me a new light
for my Schwinn bike, to make it safe at night.
It had a separate gear that touched the wheel,
and made the light rev up. It seemed unreal.

The salesman wafted honey in the breeze:
"Sir you won't need to buy him batteries."
I couldn't wait to try the new machine.
Its chrome gleamed silver on the Schwinn so clean.

After dinner, I walked it across the way
to Harding School, my grade school in the day.
The night was mine: a slave who'd done me wrong.
The school was black, the asphalt smooth and strong,

the entire playground mine, a universe
to fly around in, or a stolen purse.
Dark clung around me like a jet-black robe:
demons drew close and fondled my ear lobe.

Wild with air and coolness in the night,
I pedaled round and round and round and round,
blazing the new chrome generator light,
screaming and yelling, but without a sound.

The more I strained, the brighter it became.
The school's gray walls were glazed with yellow flame.
The night was blind, and in the valley, then,
no one could see me—it was after ten.

The town was mine, Persia at my feet,
the green paint on the slick tin bike was neat.
Warm stratus clouds silvered the moon above:
there was no need for food, or work, or love.

With all my arms and legs, and all my might,
I pedaled, pedaled, pedaled in the night.
And afterwards, when I was breathing deep,
the hero's rest soon mine alone to reap,

guiding the bike back on unsteady feet,
and all the coffee in my mind had perked,
Dad, no doubt, asked how well the light had worked.
"It worked just fine," I said. "It's really neat."

He went back to his book, and bowed his head,
and then I went upstairs, and flopped in bed.
For happiness, there was no need to pray.
It rained a lot in Oregon's gray day,

but on some nights, light took flight, anyway.

Oregon Summer

There's a red river that still seems to go
through twisting channels, though it goes so slow;
in the high summer, it's a tired snake,
and stagnant water makes the mudflats bake.

The summer leaves are glazed with heat like snow.
They almost melt, and yet they never do.
At dusk they whisper, in a foreign tongue,
out of the darkening blue in which they're hung.

Here in the cooling night, the subtle eyes
of summer stars stare in the fading skies.
The skies know something that we don't yet know.
Like eyes in masks, stars look at us. They glow.

Boys on Bikes

As lamps flick on, the sky begins to glow
with sunset greens and silver summer stars.
We ride our bikes in circles, fast and slow,
on the vast asphalt playground, free of cars.

With unbound energy and breath, I race,
laughing and screaming, braking in the dirt—
my friend, a blurred old bike and pale face—
the night air rippling in my cotton shirt.

And afterwards, I walk my bike, at rest,
to the soft, lighted houses of the town,
exertion pinned like medals to my chest,
the snake-like milky way, a silver crown.

Cascadia

Here, green things are suffused by softening sight.
The orange butterfly in the yellow shade
flickers from the dark to dark, and bright to bright,
as air bends thin-stemmed grasses, blade by blade.
In this thick whispering checkerboard of lights—
a rich susurrus under sunlit sky—
the tips of Douglas fir trees blow like kites,
beneath the wooly clouds that fly, that fly.
And as I push into the river run,
my whitened ankles tighten in the swirl,
here in this cat's eye of an afternoon,
while all the shivering minnows in the pearl
of water flick from shadow into sun,
and the sky, cobalt, cools to a crescent moon.

Hypnosis

The fresh hot smell of dry grass and rich earth
hypnotized me when I was a boy
growing up in rural Oregon.
There were so many large lawns, in old
Corvallis near the college campus, then.
I would drift over empty lawns, the quads,
with all the grass, orderly sprinklers hissing.
One could get warm on grass, out in the open,
and then cool in a sprinkler, or get warm
again standing against the wall
of a brick college building, and then cool
again in shadow. Such was the first world.
The campus always was in walking distance
of all our houses, as my father taught there,
and I achieved a yogic emptiness
from the first outset of recorded summer.
Nothing was quite as good as standing in silence,
almost alone in country or in town,
with the sound of nothing anywhere at all,
standing on brown grass in the August heat,
feeling the sun on shoulders and the neck,
and smelling everything around—air, flowers, trees,
grass and dirt, maybe wood from an old shed,
as if everything was always full
without an effort—one just had to breathe.

Hi-Fi

Airily, over the radio,
the announcer's voice throbs, cultured,
    polished, slow:
He says Dvorak's *New World Symphony.*
At least on the FM, it's here for free.

Where have I heard the melody before?—
When I was 10 and sitting on the floor
in front of Dad's sleek, newly bought hi-fi.
He had no money, and the price was high.

Now, Dvorak's pleasant; then, an ecstasy.
What leaches out from 10 to 70?
I remember Dad, once, ordered a record
that took weeks, by mail. To me, it had no chord—

just a man's untuned wailing. "What's that, Dad?"
"That's a cantor chanting." "It's sounds sad."
"It moved me when I was a kid, but now that I'm old,
it's gone. The cantor's music leaves me cold."

I couldn't believe him. There was no way how
you could like something, but not like it now.
I sat for years on the soft pine wood floor,
and spun Dad's hi-fi records, more and more.

Land

This is what it's like to be surprised
by a sight of land, gold grass, stretching to the horizon
and quiet trees—the oaks—nearby and far:

at such moments, no words—such things came long
before the tongue was free from clay and broke
the silence of the land with its sly code.

Here, all that's needed once more is the fume
of eucalyptus brush, and the heat's pulse,
while all around the smells of earth rise up,

with the far hills blurring into woods,
silvery oak leaves in their summer skin,
and the brown river's flashing golden eye.

Now, the whole self is able for a spell
to leave the equivocation of the tongue
and be complete, feet solid on the earth;

and this is it, one meaning of the place,
as the whole consciousness becomes the heat,
as if to see the land is happiness,

as if to breathe the air, an ancient rite,
beloved of animals who have no names,
until I recollect my proper name

and all the spell is broken of the heat,
and I'm just standing sweaty there again
with a self-conscious laugh ready to go,

schlepp back to the car in aging shoes
and continue the journey past colored signs.

Book II

Bennington, 1962

The summer corn hissed by the old mansion.
We ran in the upper rooms, through the old clothes—
nineteenth-century black dresses, sepia photographs:

we, the privileged boys and girls of the 60s,
running like endless alphabets through the euphoric
text of July, plunging into night

past the great windows,
past the guests, the moon and the Japanese lanterns,
past all belief onto the lawn again and again.

Vermont Summer

Move slowly through the day: the yellow wheat
rises as thick as bone in August heat.
The plants are velvety, a bee
rolls in his heavy flight from tree to tree,
buzzing around the apples, hanging, thick
with water, on each sodden apple stick.
The woods are full
of wetness—like a sunken Spanish hull;
flowers shine like wool: and there, behind the trees,
one hears cars whispering in the summer breeze.

The grass, so sweet around the house's skirts,
mixed with the smell of apples, almost hurts;
already frogs chirrup, and mosquito shoals
buzz on the door screen, blackening random holes.
Old pine wood sweats, and cotton furniture
is dank and sodden in the shadow's blur;
out the window
one can hear the combines mow
the wheat: a bright, red, mechanized platoon
chattering through the endless August noon.

The time moves like a clock on silent feet
and the wood creaks within the summer heat.
The body blurs, the sensual afternoon
turns white and brilliant, like a silk cocoon.
I wait for early dinner, as the still
dark blue grows thicker on the window sill:
light food tonight,
and then the endless silver-smithy skies
of August with a million fireflies
telling us that all things are, or should be, right.

Dinner

The subtle, vulpine moment at the dinner,
when we humiliate the honored guest,
turns sinner into saint, and saint to sinner,
by making good men equal to the rest.

The cattiness of social living rooms
reminds us of the feline in us all:
we stumble onward to our human dooms,
uncertain when our charms begin to pall.

No need to eat our neighbor's flesh, we bite
into his soul, although his pants are creased,
and then we bid him a polite good night:
he may not know he was the evening's feast.

Oriental Rug

The oriental rug—a sideways glance—
half blurs to plants and trees, or bulbs of fruit,
teapots and samovars and noses, eyes,
odd beasts, and birds in geometric rings.

The magic flash of blue, a child's trance,
this twisted fiber orange to the root,
turns gray perception into rainbow dyes,
the mind's gray blort to shapes: let there be things!

Fireflies

Ah those New England fireflies—
blinking dots of lemon, lime,
in the twilit summer skies:
beetle mania sublime.

Fireflies are a serious upper
after a warmish summer supper,
rather like perceptual spice,
following carbonnade and rice.

Shades in a lamp-lit puppet show,
they swerve in sunset's lurid glow,
their colored trails flaming arcs,
hot sparklers spitting out cool sparks.

They're art for art's sake. They just are.
We needn't pay. Each one's a star.
Does this mean things will be all right?
They'll sizzle on throughout the night.

Vermont Winter

Deep winter in Bennington: the garnet brush,
tan colored sharp grass spiking up through snow;

each breath of ice and steam; a silver flush
of silence pulsing everywhere you go;

the crunch of ones own shoes, hands turning white,
thin cheek bones tortured by the thumbscrew cold;

and coming indoors—wood in yellow light—
tearing off a coat, delicious gold

honey-sweet rush of warm air everywhere,
flowing over the skin, an ocean, there.

Mediterranean, 1965

The olive groves, the wine-blush of the sea,
the salt air, looking down from ancient cliffs
on the Mediterranean, as if blood
of the old world turned to gold in the bright sun,

gold stones and gold rough grasses underfoot
on the Mediterranean coast in the 60s:
me a gangling teenager with my parents.
We walked towards a cafe with marble floors—

through olive trees, there, then, the plinth of coolness.
The sea like Lacoon's serpent, was coiled beneath
in compact sheathes, a cobalt blue, blood red.
We sipped wine—no-one knew we were alive.

My Dad said, this is Homer's wine-dark sea,
as the sun glinted on the crinkled sea,
thousands of feet below, beneath the cliffs,
He could say it without too much irony,

letting it go, past irony, the feeling,
walking uphill with his wife on the small path,
there in late middle age, a happy day;
in sunny southern France, the olive groves

past the dry yellow grass, rough olive trees,
black-clad women going up the cobbled hills,
turning to dusk—the sea, a cobalt jewel,
liquid, coiling like intertwined snakes.

That was his gift, the oddest gift, the feeling,
letting it go, past irony, the feeling
that all experience was real, sea,
both blue and red, deep, indescribable.

This is Homer's sea, my father said,
a poor Jew from Brooklyn who had made good,
walking under the olive trees,
in the hot sun, fifty years ago;

no-one could say it for me, then, like him,
so happy, self-assured, so full of life;
as I loped behind, in my penny loafers,
and my best checked summer short-sleeve shirt.

We walked on the streets of those medieval towns
sand in the rubber sandals, on our toes,
bitten to death by olive-fat mosquitoes,
laughing or shouting at the souvenirs,

walking towards the hillside cafe, laughing,
to eat a fish lunch in our relatively happy
discomfort and quarreling. See, that was it: the feeling;
he had the gift of feeling—making it real,

like the man in the play by Camus,
who made a coffee cup real by touching it.

Book III

College

Who were the friendships of my adolescence?
I loved baroque: Antonio Vivaldi,
Domenico Scarlatti, Purcell, Handel,
fermenting hearing into effervescence;
and endless Bach, and brassy Frescobaldi.
LP records were the hot, bright candle.

Then came the British poets, freshman year.
Pope was the finest; also, Donne, Marvell;
I'd already done romantics—Wordsworth, Keats.
Blake, Burns and Shelley puzzled me like hell.
Chaucer, and Spenser, wine; some others, beer.
My soul responded to their antic beats.

I went to plays, and worshiped all the greats,
saw Burton and Olivier on stage.
The classic films in college were at nine,
and play rehearsals went till dawn—divine.
Was it my youth, or was it just the age?
In the 60s, then, it seemed the loving fates

whispered of culture, as they spun their threads.
I was drawn on, enthusiastically.
It helped me feel great and feel free—
as cars rolled through the streets on rubber treads,
and staff mopped up linoleum for me.
Those were the kinds of things I didn't see.

First Visit to England, 1967

He took the train through plush and light green hills,
just out of college, wanting to see all.
Bath was to be visited. He stayed
in a cheap hotel somewhere, and washed
his dying socks in the luxurious sink.
People still hawked meat pies on the street.
He had read the great 18th-century novels,
and saw the baths themselves that novelists
and cartoonists had grossly satirized,
when sanitation was a distant dream,
and powdered wigs and snuff were stuff for guys.
There were side trips: on a cloudy day,
he walked, delighted, to a great estate
open to the public. For a mile
large trees lined the path from the front gate,
like the ghosts of so many kind noble ladies.
He gaped, backpacked, in heat, and in grandeur—
This is the way it was supposed to be.
Ah, the great rooms, the smell of furniture,
endless porcelain, wood, and brass, and oils
of the local gentry, and their children.
Dickens, Thackeray, Tennyson lived this world,
and now I see it too. Actually.
An American dream come true—the Old World's spoils.

Oxford, 1970

Oxford, 1970: fall rain sleets
and glistens on absolutely empty streets,
at midnight. Nothing there,
but blacked-out gothic buildings everywhere.
The American student heart still beats.

Nothing like it at home, no map or marks.
At night, I sneak into centuries-old parks
hidden behind stone college walls: these larks.
It's freezing. Toes dead, icy wet, I see
a few dons walk in blackness, somberly,

moving, more furtive, hushed, than even me.
October carnival: here the very best ride
is the electric mini-cars, which bump
one another with bone-jarring thump.
The neon lights are garish, and the pallid
teens run around, a tossing, red-haired salad.

God, the fog, so thick, which comes so near
really is like pea soup, obscuring neat
prim shop facades along each college street.
People are bitter. Everything is dear.
At morning, we have sunset's twilight gloom.
To warm my graduate student room,

I have to put a shilling in the plug:
thirty minutes of electricity, per slug.
God, the cold—go to a pub, have rows
of fries and overdone steak—then, as the rain blows
past denuded medieval endless trees,
walk by closed butcher shops whose windows

host pigs' heads with pipes and tweed caps. Wow.
A jolly come-on. Who would I be to judge
the time or place at this point, or to nudge
the reality into some picture frame.
In any event, it's gone forever now.
The world has changed. I saw the end of same.

New York Summer

The gaudy summer effloresces cool—
in day-glo yellows, greens, papaya pink—
strolls down the street, a cat, licking itself,

branding the hoods of old Chevys with fire,
jittering brown grass in parks—old man summer.
Summer walks down the street like a stray cat.

Sweltering kids play in the spraying hydrant.
Steam rises from grates, fogging glasses;
sweat drenches my shirt, underwear, socks.

Wait till the night, the night of ash, when the city,
its sky orange at midnight, rises swollen
by midsummer, windows blinking and flaring,

the moon over the city yellow neon,
the cats calling to one another in back,
while the ashes of past lives, metallic, acrid,

blow through the bedroom window onto the sheets.

Marijuana, 1970

New York subway:
white tiles, arches,
deep Babylon.
I drifted to
arcades, endless mirrors
of dancing girls:
weed-palate,
wandering through
subway arches—
Arabian knights'
porcelain miles—
boy in Disneyland.
The ragged clutched seats.
I stumbled by them,
an armored saint.
Stoplights' cellophane
lit silky curtains of
rain on Amsterdam
as I staggered
to my rented room
feeling profound
absorption of self
by heavy things:
street, lamps, rooms,
sitting like conscious
chess pieces on
a magic board.

Birdhouse, Bronx Zoo

Tropical birds float in the dappled glow
of summer sun. A tentacle of air
shivers their feathers as they dart below,
like lizards, to the shallows of their lair.

Stuttering flux and soft explosions hit
the vacant ear, and endless flickering jewels—
of emeralds, rubies, purple agates, spit
into white light. Wings throb like waves in pools.

Framed by the sun and heat, they sit and stare.
The parrots and the toucans sharply preen,
chattering syllables of blatant air,
and shudder yellow, pink, and black and green.

A hoard of treasure forged at no expense,
jewelry box of alabaster eyes,
turned into beings by the human sense,
they glitter, glitter under noontime skies.

Presents

I wandered in the glittering world
of New York stores for many years,
as woven Christmas goods unfurled
on polished, plush mahogany tiers,

looking at silken luxuries—
scarves for Mom, and ties for Dad.
It felt warm in the winter freeze.
Sometimes they were a little sad,

and I was happy at the thought
a Christmas gift could give them glee;
as if, once chosen, and once bought,
a spark of light would set them free.

Ties for him and scarves for her:
they thanked me then and seemed amused.
He was a little fussier.
She liked the way the colors fused.

After he died, I went to Greece
and bought a broach, a bee of gold,
for Mom. It wasn't golden fleece—
but by then she'd gotten old—

and wore it, as she said, for me.
They loved fine art and culture. This
touched her heart, the buzzing bee
of a marriage's small bliss,

when I wandered in her garden
and she watched with hope new won
that life had granted her a pardon,
and I'd be a loving son.

The Writer

His doom came on early—when he went to college.
He had a professor who thought he was smart.
That was the source of his love of knowledge:
he took the man's good nature, too much, to heart.

He moved to the city. He had a great vision,
the glory that moved him—a novel, or book.
He couldn't think of it with total precision,
but somehow it grew on him, and it just took.

He wrote, and he read, and he wrote and he wrote,
with pencil and typewriter through the short day,
ignoring his shoes, and threadbare wool coat.
His mother sent money and cookies his way.

Each gray flannel dork he met showed him his own grace.
Pizza suited his tongue, and played his head tune.
He loved the New York Public Library space;
fame could find him right there, and it might find him soon.

He took to a small bar and went there quite late.
His only friend was the sad-eyed Spanish waiter.
He didn't know whether the place was that straight;
but he'd worry about such trivia later.

Forty years passed. The world in its glory,
seedy, obtuse, with each flesh-colored dawn,
passed slowly by. Each man has a story,
but he had his chess game and savaged each pawn.

One day, he dropped dead at the bar. With police,
the janitor entered his place, and surveyed,
in search of a rolodex, or a signed lease.
The mother was dead. He left, slightly afraid.

The body was sent to the morgue, and unclaimed.
The thousand-page manuscript went to the trash.
Young man, if you don't want to die, thus, unnamed,
don't go for the writing; seek fun, friends and cash.

Scholarship

Sartre wrote that scholarship
is what clerks write about what clerks
have written since the dawn of time:
like ever-youthful soda jerks
offering Classic Coke, with lime,
on the deck of a sinking ship.
Writing about one's thoughts about
whatever the previous scholarly
commentator wrote to rout
the scholar who wrote about the great
writer keeps scholars up quite late.
It's better, far, than mere TV.

The Great Man

For fifty years, his voice rose in kind greeting,
in academic conference and meeting:
judicious, wise, quite subtle, and alert.

A child of culture—and a charming flirt—
he had smart students, offered food and cheer
at his wife's table, once or twice a year.

He's gone now. His memory, vivid at first, grows less.
His finest students, older, with each stress
accommodate a quickly changing world.

Great was his intellect, a mind unfurled.
He had finesse, humanity, and range;
but others came along—it's hardly strange

that virtually all that's left now is an entry
in Wikipedia, 500 words set free.

Old Professor

He warbles on about the Renaissance,
tells stories of the 50s, in Provence,
long, languid days under the Spanish sun,
a visit with Picasso—oh what fun—
deconstructs Botticelli's *Saint Sebastian,*
illuminates how great cathedrals fan.
The old professor still warms many hearts.
But what they don't see is the flickering darts
that stung, in silence, over 80 years—
a mother who succumbed to icy fears,
students whose boasted sex lives mocked his own,
the wife whose real friend was on the phone,
bored summers in Maine, a drug-addicted son,
the younger dean who challenged him, and won.
People have cocktails with him. Watch him think.
But watch out for the second whisky drink.
That's when the anger flows, too fast, and loose.
They leave before he kills the golden goose.

Book IV

Sunset

My God, look at this Canaletto sky
over this mundane city—Washington—
a moment of transcendence in the eye,
flickering from the done to the undone.

Suddenly, the old chords of my mind
chime once, and then they chime a second time,
as if there's sweetness in the summer wind,
these clouds of strawberry—this sky of lime.

Beyond here, fishes shiver in the sea.
The moon casts tarnished silver on their skin.
The clouds are dying ghosts, then, velvety,
the night moves Eastward to the room I'm in.

Kingdom of Blueberries

This is the kingdom of blueberries, here by the river:
vineyards, ladies in gowns sparkling with silver;
and the red deer, chased by huntsmen and horses
with blue silk trappings like plum petals.
Myrrh, aloes and cinnamon grow in clover.
All the geese are made of marzipan,
the hens' eggs full of sweet cream. Underneath
the mica-light blueberry sky of winter,
shivering red-faced boys and girls on skates
fall into powdered sugar, laughing at nothing.
A subtle richness fills all with happiness,
and the light laughter can be heard from fields.
Navigators, wearing snow-white blouses
sail craft upriver, laughing, in the sun spray
to where mountains hang over cities, like blue silk.

Lavender

Vaguely unfolding in the broadened band
of the light sky West, it is lavender,
strengthening over dark-topped roofs and land,
infiltrating salmon-pink sky, the blur

of the remaining rain clouds; what a moment;
looking at sunsets all my life, I've never
actually seen pure lavender, a portent
of something—riches, joy, and fame, maybe, this New Year;

deeper, more liquid than the finest art,
over the totally unreal green
of sunset sky, it fades, a beating heart,
briefly alive; this won't again be seen.

Village, India

This is the dry land of a thousand eyes.
In every hut, there are a million flies.
The dry land reaches to the watery sky:
the sky is as blue as is a sailor's eye.
An odor of excrement is in the air,
thin, and dried out, amounting to despair.
The gods intone over the weary earth
endless cycles of suffering, and rebirth.
A boy stands in the shade with a dark stare.
A girl walks quickly in the village glare.
The women's silks are rich with peacock dyes,
and flow like wings of sun-drenched butterflies.
Great granite monoliths can testify
to long gone truths that turned into a lie.
Who can say who lives, or thrives, or dies?—
for this is the dry land of a thousand eyes.

India

Temple

Yellow dust dances in sun.
Carmine statues curve in air,
smiling faces, slanting eyes,
stem-like waists, petal legs.
The temple is metallic blue.
Elephant feet, brass-ornamented,
loaf in the shade of lime green trees.

Back of the Taj

At six o'clock, the land's gray cloth,
soft fields under river silt.
Clumps of black trees stretch to blur.
Across the sanded flats, on gold,
the red fort stands, a stony mass
smudged by the smoke. A rowboat creeps
along a thread. Day vanishes.

Vinalhaven

For the Smiths

Chestnuts still spring from trees like silent elves,
and beds of squash swell near a withered barn;
rainwater drips through moss's subtle sieves,
and mushrooms turn their slime to silky yarn.

The handled wood is smooth and silver-gray,
pine needles whisper in a humid wind,
paint flakes from boards, and gleams in scattered hay—
and fallen apples wither in green rind.

Dense razor grass forks up from the whitened stone,
small flowers creep on vines beside a tree;
old branches bleach, and turn as white as bone;
the only sounds are wind and bumblebee.

Capri

The ocean fades into the pearls and grays
inside a conch shell. Sea and sky are one,
with mild, understated taste, the days
now blurring into something without sun

so different from New England dusk—no flames
no icy northern skies—as if the rye
and corn of eons, children's marble games,
for centuries, polished the clouds and sky.

Here I can almost see insect-like
triremes setting sail on the dark.
Above, sparse pine frets on a shadowed spike,
a peak with the old palace and its park.

Tiberius had rule and sway of life
and death of men and women amid falls
of pools and flowers, in the darkened pines,
where the bird with its old Latin name still calls.

The ancient groves, above the rocks that leach
their reflux and destruction in the dusk
from water, now tempt chaos into speech,
next to flowering tree and silent husk,

as I sit upon the terrace, bathed and choired:
Be human smell the citrus, feel free,
drink or make love, or hate—or be inspired,
for in this ancient garden by the sea,
everything human's known, and is required.

Greece

Here is a silver synopsis where waves whisper
from the Aegean blowing on the shore.

In Olympia, sunlight gilds the shards
of wrecked stone temples under olive trees

amidst red and white flowers where Zeus walked,
by cypresses, with whirring bumblebees.

ii.

I gawk in the center of the stadium
under a vortex of blue sky, and climb

silky marble bleachers in the theater
of Epidaurus, high above the plain;

a worn, curved armrest on a marble seat
is all that's left of someone's memory.

iii.

Now I can stand on top of the citadel
at Mycenae where Agamemnon lived

and died and look down at the wild valley
he looked out on the day he left for Troy.

iv.

This place, so drowned in ancient darkness, loss,
and golden light, seems like a long-lost home,

and the Aegean, a diamond necklace,
that's always been here, laughing in the sun.

Olympia

The old stone archway leads to the green field—
so I drift through, escaping the tour group,
and find myself Olympic Stadium.
There are only a few tourists wandering.
This ancient place is almost mine alone.
My God, the sun is hot, the sky, a flare,
tearing at pale skin, covered with sunblock.
So this is it? This place? Olympia,
here in Greece, for real? What could be nicer?—
lapis sky, oval field, grassy slopes—
once marble benches—red and white small flowers,
leading to trees—good God, what could be nicer?
Thick column masses of the shrine of Zeus
can still be touched. The granite burns in sun;
the smell of hot stone sends me to the sky.
What joy this is. Here now. This place. It is:
the heat, the smells, the stone, the shade, the trees.
Surely their gods were good. One feels it still.
Gods differ in place and time. They had good gods.

Lisbon Art Museum

This is the kingdom of peaches,
grand melting of silk,
cream silk over the porcelain
ancient Chinese vases,
peaches on etched trees.

The perfect oil paintings
shimmer, crème brulée—
rich burnt sugar skins of
white vanilla cream.

Women's summer dresses
reflect their metal glitter
on the polished floors.

Outside, stones are sweet,
because they are the yellow
lemons, sisters of peaches.

The sun shines in white drops
of liquor-like perfumes,
and the darting flight
of bright eyes like leaves.

The Grand Mosque of Cordoba

I see sweet oranges
in gardens with dark green leaves
in Cordoba. Red dust

coats hedges. Everywhere
small alleys, manic threads,
scatter shells of white walls,

opening to courtyards,
gel-like flowers and trees
shimmering through barred gates.

Here rises the Grand Mosque.
I approach wall and door—
lines, geometric, snake

on pastel silky tiles—
enter the watery shadow
through the gilt arch and see

glittering bays on the ceiling:
universes of colored stars
drift silent into light.

Endless pulses of arches
recede to infinity,
all-knowing void of air,

arches on arches and
endless layers of pillars,
and fire-bejeweled walls.

All sits and waits,
a magic shadow of time—
echoing endless words.

Caballero

They tried to cheat me in Seville,
or they were careless, on one line:
I ordered a single glass of wine.
They put a bottle on the bill.

I could feel my face turning red,
pointing it out to the waitress.
As usual, I'd been well fed.
She didn't show the least distress.

"Excuses to the caballero,"
is how she put it, in her rush
back to the bar, to change a zero,
as I let go the startled flush.

As in a dream, I saw it all:
the shadow self I might have been,
with cape, and sword, adroit, thin,
on a white horse—admired, tall.

By the time she got back, the trip
was over. She had met my need.
I paid her, with a padded tip,
and left, exulting at their greed.

Post-Inquisition

I don't understand Spanish well,
but get enough of it to be able
to know, when my Cordoba hotel
calls to reserve a dinner table,
the girl's being asked about my name.
"Jewish," she says, as if that's a slight fame.

Cordoba—the heart—and pride
of the Spanish Inquisition.
Now, of course, it's swept aside,
by brooms, secular disquisition.
As I exit the hotel, alone,
eager to see the wizardry of the medieval stone

outside where gold sunbeams glow,
I smack into the glass front door.
The staff's concerned, simpatico,
as I bleed on the white marble floor.
The woman at the hotel bar goes
to get a large ice bucket, for my injured nose.

By six, nose iced, I'm feeling well.
Dinner is in the trellised mesh
of an elegant patio's twilight spell.
The waiter says the flounder's fresh.
What's it called? "Sir, we call it
Flounder in the Jewish Style."

I pause and watch the candle flit.
He looks at me, with an attentive smile.

Inheritor

The bubbles in the teacup on the table
of the verandah flicker with the ripple
of fish that shiver in the concrete pond
in the garden of this French hotel, so fond
of some Americans who die to dine.
Downtown in Tours, I walk and mull the wine;
students, desultory—so young—still leaf
their books within this sultry ancient fief.
Beneath October trees, the yellow
last sun on leaves fades to something like snow.

We take the tour, and go see the chateaux.
Like frosted cakes, the chateaux come and go
along the Loire, where spurs
of flowery bushes, hay, and winy lures
of withered hedges with suggestive vine
glow like bronze Roman coin.
(Their oxen plowed the fields of the Loire,
before the French created France, or *gloire*.)
We park by this chateau:
 it sparkles like a peacock. Then we go.

Very lucky weather this October.
This evening, on the hotel porch, and near
the fishpond (do they eat these?),
the waiter offers grapes, some wraps of cheese.
And then to dinner, where a sautéed crumb
of turnip leaves me drunk, and dumb,
in acknowledgment of the superior French.
Near here, poor plodded on in winter's clench,
and Louis often ruled a living hell;
but, casual wanderers, we inherit well.

Book V

The Shrunken Men

In the 50s and 60s I met so many older
men who had had great oceanic lives,
seen unspeakable things in World War II,
adventuring through horror and desolation,
totally alone in youth, yet finding love,
ultimately reading libraries of books—
some of whom—psychiatrists, teachers, writers—
were able to speak about this to the young
who had ears that listened for other universes,
fine-tuned, like radio telescopes. They were the last
group I knew who seemed to have significant
lives, the way life should be, a whole
universe, a story, like a novel.
Now it's as if people are plastic toys,
manufactured by TV, walking around
with one hand on the partner, and the other
on the cell phone, almost unaware
of anything except one other body,
and the application Apple has to share.

Kabuki

One of the things about being in a place
is that it becomes its own map, like a face;

so Washington for me, and so I know
a hill in the city where tree branches blow

around gigantic mansions of the rich.
I'm not among them—maybe that's a bitch—

but I used to jog there in the heat,
and silken pavement, of the flowered street.

One morning, I saw a girl who wore
a nurse's costume exit a back door.

The white stone mansion gleamed so spaciously;
its cherry trees swayed lightly, graciously.

She looked exhausted, face a painted mask
of saddened resignation to the task.

The wordless houses and the trees around
were great ships setting sail, with no sound.

Probably not one neighbor even knew
who still lived in the house, or just a few.

She must have worked the night shift, in the heat.
The nurse walked downhill in the empty street,

to catch her bus on the main avenue.
I had to jog on home and fix my shoe.

What misery lurked behind the stucco wall?
It could be almost anything at all—

as if the wealthy houses were just thin
white paper screens, with shadow-forms within.

The silent nurse peeled the golden rind:
sudden kabuki theater of the mind.

Fête Champêtre

Ah to be in a fête champêtre,
of 18th-century bien-être,
a pastel park by Fragonard,
an antique vision, yet unmarred.

Here in the dark museum room,
gold light steals through the gloom:
young men and women dine, and dance,
a fantasy of regal France,

on arcing lawns with endless space,
billowing trees that flow like lace,
a sky of strawberry and cream,
fountains that gild the silver stream.

Ah, to be healthy and be young,
when lutes are struck, and songs are sung:
immortal young aristocrats,
intense, undone silk-coated cats.

The sky casts checkered sun and shade
on languid statues, lightly frayed,
crumbling arches—music's measure,
fruit and wine—the second's pleasure.

What blushing women, loved by clowns,
lounge in loose, rich silken gowns?
Now candlelit, an old Pierrot
plucks a lute, in this Watteau.

Come night, the torches fire bright
to highlight comedy's low light:
with colored masks, the masque infers
the chiaroscuro characters.

At the end, like powdered sugar spray,
the glittering sweetness blows away,
whipped cream spilled from silver spoon
before the tongue can taste—too soon.

Lady With Unicorn Tapestry,
Museum of Cluny, Paris

Her eyes peep, coy, out of a formal pose,
eyebrows thin plucked amidst a wall of rose
after five hundred years. White trees and flowers
leap from the silk, and beasts in woven bowers
flicker between the beastlike and human,
a man's eyes whimpering in prancing lion.

Who knows who first designed, and wove the thread:
the pallid skin, the gleaming blue and red
of sleeves and headdresses, a unicorn
that comes to court, be courted, with a horn.
The white beast, hypnotized by its eyes, above,
glimpsed in her mirror, frozen in self-love.

Small slips list symbols of the human senses
in the medieval garden close that fences
chaos in form: not hard to understand.
The sensual symbolism is quite grand.
The lion ramps, and jewel-like flowers riot.
Taste, touch, and hearing are alive, if quiet.

Did the unicorn really love the lady?
The thought dusts pinkish powder on the rose
sewn in the garden, after 500 years.
Certainly, they'll never be that close.
Even a white beast can provoke black fears:
dainty, despising love, forever ready.

Our lives may be much nicer than those dead
who wore their fingers as they loomed blood red.
We're more exact; and yet, the ancient feeling,
the spark of gold and ruby, still revealing
the grand, gilt visions of the Renaissance,
is our woven shirt, our provenance.

The Escape

The sun on the forest turns gold in the breeze,
and drifts down seaward, lighting sparks in trees.
In the bay, my sail ships look like small flies,
laden with oil, gold for foreign eyes.
I never thought for a moment I'd be here
in this port city, free of pain and fear,
in my own house with light on polished floors,
with a wife to mind my manners, and my mores.
No, when young, I thought I'd be the slave
of great Achilles, well, until the grave.
Achilles—half-generous, half-snot;
I officered his shirt, and chamber pot.
When the commander took his girlfriend, he
screamed for days, like a crazed, stormy sea.
And so emotional—all sweaty, dazed—
dragging his foe—his eyes unfocused, glazed
an atrocity, all knew, and crazy thing;
yet, he returned the body to the king.
Had a stray point not pierced his naked heel,
he'd still be with me; and I'd make his meal.
But his luck ended, and the wound turned black.
You can't avoid Death, though you turn your back.
No use by then to pound, or scream, or pout;
Death was unmoved, and his great breath ran out.
And now I hear things, songs—a golden boy—
son of the goddess, at the gates of Troy,
blinding his friends and foemen with his face,
hurling the spear with godlike force and grace.
The war was won entirely by committee;
it was a trick that sacked the Trojan city.

Well, lucky me, as sad Troy burned, I took
off my slave tokens, and I changed my look,
snuck into one of the last boats to leave,

hauled on the rope, and strained, and didn't grieve;
then landed here, and found a master who
taught me my numbers, and some letters too.
And Achilles, well, I knew his joy and pain,
but if I told, they'd think that I'm insane.
His life was short and yes, he gained a prize.
I see his legend growing, in their eyes—
now he's a spirit, gleaming in the sky,
a star in heaven, searing the night sky.
No man can compass him or match his worth.
The real man was molded of the earth.

How strange—last night he came, as in a dream,
laughing, ironic, with his eyes agleam,
as he was when he was still quite young,
and seemed amused to hear his praises sung.
"I always liked you, Argurios," he said.
"You had something going in your head.
While others quaffed, and stared, and sat, and japed,
you kept busy and found things to do.
And finally, when Dame Fortune winked at you,
and they died there—clever boy, you escaped."

Priest

Two men accusing me, and I do not
even remember them. They see themselves,
still, as athletic teens, who think they're hot,
seductive with both sexes—friendly elves.

Now of course, they're different—they don't see:
sagging and balding, bitter, hairy, failed.
They're not the shining youth they seemed to be,
charming and ignorant, who Mary hailed.

How sad, the common fate. The thin cocoon
breaks and the caterpillar trips about.
Snakes shed their skin, and writhe beneath the moon,
and crabs molt shells and skitter sideways out.

And boys, who seem eternal, too, are shells.
All crack the shell, as I did—from within.
A tense, embittered man crawls out, and swells,
chained to submission, and a sense of sin.

Your failed job, your bank account, your wife?
You don't see that it's none of my affair.
Extorted money won't give you new life.
You'll find it vanishes, and turns to air.

Unwritten Poems

Unwritten poems are fiddlehead ferns,
sprouting in tall grass, curling by turns,
or ammonite fossils, shells deep in a rock,
never to wind out, life frozen in shock.

They are atoms of mindfulness, every small thing
that passes through sense and takes form, starts to sing:
the wave of first feeling, spray of words, leach
and foam of all language, laced out on a beach.

Every one feels inspired, no doubt,
but has not the symbols to write it all out—
endless life, endless passion, intense, everywhere—
invisible ink that dissolves, into air.

Nemerov

The last time I saw Howard Nemerov
was for such an odd reason—I had been
a civil servant in hot Washington
for several years, and he had come here too
to be Poet Laureate, with a very grand
office in the Library of Congress.
I went to visit. He offered to buy me lunch,
not because I knew him, but because
he had been a colleague of my father,
who had died a few years before. So he took me
to a small, plush, lunch place, and we talked
desultorily, since we really didn't
know one another all that well. After,
we walked, together, uphill towards the Court,
and, without thinking, I increased my pace,
worried about getting back to work.
"Slow down, Paul," he said, in that soft, wry, voice.
"You're still young. You have a place to go.
It's different for me. I'm already there."

Ring

Well, I just had my own seventieth
birthday, and I thank those who came,
and helped me to celebrate—and bought the wine.
Thank you for showing me such courtesy.
Now, a week or two later, I lay down
this afternoon, to take a nap. I dreamed
I was a kid again, and camping out,
as I did in several still remembered Junes,
paid for, of course, by a kind hearted Dad,
first on the West coast, later in the East,
snuggling in a tight cotton sleeping bag
in a group tent amid a vast black night—
and, all around, the sharp, sharp smell of pine
and rain, the flapping canvas of the tent,
the padded cotton of the sleeping bag,
as I fell off into sun-stunned sleep.
For a moment, time itself seemed to fold up—
unfolding back to city, work, and age—
the years between, a forest of dry brush,
consumed by leaping flames, in a vast instant.
So the kid's world of the summer camp
merged with the present, and uncertain streets—
a fiery gleam, a gold ring on a hand.

Autumn

Everything is being dialed down,
a world of boiling blues becoming still,
quieting into grays, and pewter clouds.
The white light lies, weak, on a window sill.

The body's easier, because it can move fast
in coolness down the sidewalk, with no need
for greasy sunblock, pools of sticky sweat,
as skin-peeling sun starts to recede.

Some like it cool. The world around me spins
into an orange night, the sugared glee
of childhood's Halloween, and a blood moon
will rise at ten—a phantom strawberry.

People begin to layer, take the shape
of seeds turning into pods, extruding shells,
and become oval as they walk along.
The autumn leaches into leaf mold smells.

A few Japanese lanterns sway in the dusk:
faces of teachers, parents, who smile at me,
who make fall joyful. I feel their candle warmth.
As I walk on, the past's in front of me.

The Pen

In fourth grade Rome my pen became a fright,
leaking bright blue black ink on every shirt.
I hated math. Dad forced me to learn,
drilling me in multiplication tables,
so next year, back in America I'd be
ready—whatever happened in fifth grade.
Roman history was much easier.
There was something: violent gladiators,
tortures, wars, ancient Etruscan tombs,
and lions eating saints in the arena,
that spoke quite nicely to my fourth grade soul.
Cicero, Ceasar, Pompey, Crassus, Sulla
seemed like the grownups you would want to meet,
sensational people who, once known, would always
be your champion—and make you friends.
On weekends, Dad took me to a bluff that looked
over the railroad yards, so I could see
the engines and the trains. We sometimes passed
a little man with a cart who sold pens
and packs of letter paper on a side street.
So one sunny Sunday, Dad, relaxed,
said "Okay, let's go. I'll get you the new pen."
He loved the ancient place, the atmosphere,
and felt somewhat sorry for the little man,
eking a living after World War II,
smiling and nodding as we walked along.
Dad happily bargained with him. Finally,
he took out a luxurious blue velvet case
and showed us a pen he swore was a Parker.
I held it in my hand and said okay.
Mom's precious Parker needed special ink.

Dad wasn't ready for that, and when we left
explained the pen was a knockoff, probably
made in Japan; but anyway, it worked.
And so, the dripping solved, I carried on
trying to learn multiplication tables
piling up like giant ziggurats
in notebook squares. I'd rather have watched rats
eating the bodies of defeated slaves,
while I licked chocolate bars on marble thrones.
Dad took me to museums, sometimes movies,
and always gave me books, the kind, unspoken
invisible links to wit and fantasy.
Back home, the pen's blue ink line widened soon
from math to other things, new words, new thoughts,
and then became a Tiber flowing through
a widening city, spilling out to sea.
As I went from grade to grade, then on to college,
it turned into an ocean, on which
my boat still sails, heading into port.

Moth and Bluebird

There's a tattered brown moth on the window
of my bedroom, trying to get out.
He flaps futilely against the glass.
He reminds me of my father in his brown overcoat,
dead 30 years ago, but still beloved.
Please Dad, I think, don't die, get out, get out.
Here, I'll open the window, pry the screen
so you can fly out—fly into the air.
Be happy Dad, don't mind your life, don't die
from that botched heart surgery and the pain;
go out into the blue and the sun, be free,
relishing life, joking, full of hope
as you were young. May you be free forever.

As I walk down the street, I see a beautiful
bluebird sitting on a flowery bush.
That's my mother's soul: she looks at me
with a mild peck, and then flies off,
with the sharp hint of wings and some concern.
When I was a boy, she would sometimes say
"Look, there's a bluebird,"—like a hidden gift.
She doesn't need me any more, she has
the flowers, white as bursts of cotton here,
and the other birds, silk scarves in the sky.

Harvard Square

I look down from my hotel winter window
onto the Cambridge corner after dark
comes early, and I see the traffic pulse
while shop signs glow: yellows, whites, oranges.
The car, and bus lights are a carousel
of moving, flittering jewels in the snow,
winding around the corner in the purple
of the New England Christmas. I came here
when I was about 16, and used to like
hanging out on Harvard Square, admiring
sleek preppy, Harvard men, their intense girls.
I wanted to be one of them, part of the world
of adult cool, knowledge, sophistication.
Now, I'm 70, and, of course, my parents
who insisted that I constantly read books,
encouraged dreams of art, and scholarship,
are buried in Mount Auburn, close to here.
The undergraduates look like small kids
in wilted wet hoods, and a group of bums
camps in front of the Coop. Yet, all in all,
this place hasn't changed that much. The glowing jewels
of traffic on the wetness of the street
are what was then, and what has come of it.
I learned some parts of what they hoped I'd learn:
one only sees a fraction of the whole.
And so my parents and their friends are gone,
and the new people, moving, unaware,
of what seems like their history to me,
stumble through snow, alone, or laughing, talking.

Thanksgiving

I took my morning walk Thanksgiving day,
out from the building in downtown D.C.,
in the unsurprising temperate sun.
There were a few maples on the corner
that had turned—orange, mustards, thick blood tones.
I remember high school up in Vermont,
where there were mountains of sparking, painted trees
each fall, blurring sight sideways, as I walked,
watching for bullies, dogs, on the dirt roads,
trudging, half enchantedly, to school.
Here, the leaves are more matte, slightly dark,
with black spots at this time of year, still moist,
and rich, deep colors for a day or two.
These trees are old, trunks channeled, gnarled, and tall.
The leaves breathed, tumbled, microscopic kites,
in the balmy swell of corner wind—
as if from the perspective of the grown,
so many things had turned from work, to play,
as I went to the store, and bought a pumpkin pie.

Trees

Even in late fall, there are green leaves
in the trees in this old district, still a few
bleached garden plots, around the townhouse stone:
the leaves—dark green, pine green, blond green, blue green—
on spidery branches lacing under late
Indian summer, turquoise, midday sky.
Old oaks grow here, soot darkened giant elms,
with tangled skeins of leaves, chaotic blobs
like great soft nets—or waves of pulsing green.
How smooth the noon light is, a honey sun
flowing through the eyes, into the mind,
and down from there into the lungs and feet,
feet that walk, happy, on the dappled ground.
Someone called trees our cousins—I'd say, parents,
as if put here to tell us why we're here,
with whistling whispers almost understood.

Dawns

This glassy purity, translucent stain
of morning through the January window,
with light blue and light pink on the ice shards
of windows in far buildings, rectangles
of stone, steel and glass, tan, red, or gray,
under the thickening dawn, lasts just a pulse.
There is no solid edge where things don't change.
Dawn is a multi-colored mirror floating
in quick, cold air, due soon to disappear.
It reminds me of similar winter dawns
in Rome of more than sixty years ago:
the color of hope, of cold, smoke, light, and school,
as I got dressed, ready to walk with Dad
down the benumbed street to the school bus stop
over cobbles full of shards of greens
and orange peels: yesterday's food stalls.
Dawn had been there for millennia
seen by schoolboys, semi-civilized.
D.C. was just wilderness unseen
a few short centuries ago, when it
was silhouette tree hills, skies, and forest land.
Rome's dawn, like this, here, now, was urban squares
and rectangles, of concrete and of stone,
apartment windows' lemon-yellow lamps,
glimpsed in other peoples buildings, and
rose sparks flaring clouds of brazier smoke,
as old men roasted chestnuts on the curb.
Each day, I got on the bus, just hopeful that
I'd be able to do multiplication,
that snakelike world of numbers, but my soul
loafed in the colors, and the smells of breakfast
coming from shops, Vespas ratcheting corners.

Bees

Here is the summer wind where the leaves swell
layered, and honeysuckle near the shed
draws slugs, small blobs with feelers, to ooze by
the flower patch, near peels of white paint.
Bees bubble up from air, and wallow, dive,
circle—black, yellow, striped—small blurred bright bits
of cellophane emitting a sharp trill.
We speak of danger, dagger-like intent;
but here they somersault within a realm
of pointillism, multicolored dots
of tendrils, and leaf speckles, and of grass.
They hum, like muted strings, the rise and fall
of Debussy or Mahler. Now the cat,
his fur in tangles, flowing like a snake,
slithers low past them with his orange hair,
flicking his head to see what might arrive
for him to stalk, tense silence on white paws.
In the shed's shadow swells the living hive,
inverted pyramid, beneath the eaves.
In what small chamber, to Minoans known,
does the queen labor with her myrmidons
to gild their honeyed cells? Thin misted blood,
they swarm and glitter in the dying sun.
This is the summer of the afternoon,
a sleeper's draught, a disappearing sound.

Botanic Garden

You can feel the different textures with the mind—
thick plump rubbery leaves, or frilly moist
lacy thin wings of ferns, smooth agave stalks,
the candy colors licked up by the eyes.
Vines string for miles, pythons with no ends,
and elephant ears so tissue-like, if touched
an elephant might recoil; orchids, lithe,
half-airy sugary excrescences,
melt up, spooned ice cream from another world.
Cactuses: purses, pins, and hollow tubes,
jive on beds of sand, an ancient dance
too slow to see, immobile to our sight.
Succulents, thick and oval, children's hands
dangle upwards, to grasp light and sun.
Lakes of invisible water run like blood
through the tissues of the garden; and the scent
that brings us back to the beginning is
thick mist from granite ponds in silver heat.
Bubbles of wet moss hug damp slate, like feet.
Leaf patterns float, small kites beneath the dome.
Pastels are everywhere, intense bright inks.
A living palace melts into the air.

Modern

Grasping at walkers, bottled oxygen,
the wealthy cultured—well dressed, women, men—
enter the building that's now just for them,
the great glass art museum, urban gem.
Donors all, they're just receiving thanks,
and the Director shakes hands with the ranks,
as the sun labors downward like a spoon,
dipping into the thick-hued afternoon.
They file into a dim lecture hall,
and grope for seats, they can grope at all.
The lecturer is anything but grave,
and doesn't strain to lift his voice, or rave,
presenting Modern painting, all the latest—
Picasso, Braque, Cézanne—the newest, greatest,
with some clever theories, quite his own,
uttered in a cheery baritone.
Wanting to be told what they were told,
and then forgot, when college was a bore,
they sip that milkshake they once sipped, once more.
The lecturer's insights, neatly phrased, unfold:
and oh, Matisse's colors are a bawd.
It's such a pleasure, even when one's old—
one can still be quite challenged, even awed,
and slightly conscious of a place and time
when one had lithe, young friends, and felt sublime.
Afterwards, they stoop at the buffet,
to cheese puffs, the fat pot roast, and the tray
of custard tarts, with lemon bits on top.
Well, it's too late to sing, and dance, and hop.

The best to hope for is that things won't stop
too soon, and that they'll soon have more small, bright
artichoke quiche, and flan, and lemon tarts,
to warm hard-working, kind, and cultured hearts,
before the night, before the night, before the night.
As they exit, in the blackness, with great tone,
art deco Negroes drum and xylophone.

Book VI

Curse on an Author

May the Pushcart Prize roll right on by,
your agent be a Judas goat;
the critic make your hopes rise high,
and with his last word, slit your throat.

May the Nobel Prize be rumored twice,
but given to someone else who's bats;
may your translations, low in price,
in Paris stalls, be food for rats.

May that writing student, nice and smart,
whose hand you shook once, when enthused,
go to the dean, and, for her part,
say she felt fondled, and abused.

And may that recent spike in sales
of your first hardback, dear to you,
be to one evil ten-year-old,
who likes to sniff and lick the glue.

May your children, all their feelings pouring,
tell Oprah your new thriller's boring;
and your digital editions,
(bought in airport lounge conditions),

vanish into empty air,
locked up by Russian ransomware.

The Ballad of Disrespect

It was in Merrie England.
Two lads were on the road.
They saw a slow old man ahead,
tripped him, and spilled his load.

" Sir Wrinkle," said the bolder,
"Are you crawling to your grave?
How much gold did you ever grub;
how many boys deprave?"

The old man looked scared, and startled.
They snatched his purse and ran.
He yelled after them and cursed them.
They laughed at the old man.

A bit further along, they came upon
a gentleman dressed in green.
He had a red beard, and a great cape,
with a rich silken sheen.

"Ah what an honor it is," he said,
"to meet two such as you:
two fine, upstanding gentlemen.
I assure you, there are few.

"Let me proffer my services,
since the day is getting old;
it's somewhat distant to the town,
and the night is rumored cold.

"There's a jolly inn around the bend,
and a pretty maid there too;
two spirited lads like you will like
the inn's amusing crew."

106

The man in green had a slight limp.
One thought to jibe him weak.
But a second glance at the man in green
made him afraid to speak.

They walked with him, as in a dream,
to the inn's wood door;
then turned around, but he was gone.
He'd vanished just before.

The door sprung open, and a young
host, with a wisp of beard,
gave cheerful welcome. They relaxed,
and forgot all they had feared.

Out came the dice, the cards, the beer.
They drank, and played, and drank.
Unseen, the sun soon disappeared;
bright candles filled the blank.

They played and played. It was getting late.
Their new friends were great fun.
But the lads were in a tired state.
Their evening was all done.

"Wait," said the host. "You can't leave now.
We've won your bag of gold.
You owe the barman anyhow.
Your lives are pledged, and sold."

The oldest stood, and pushed on past.
Out came the flashing daggers.
Both boys are stabbed, chill, sharp and fast;
one falls, the other staggers.

And, as he dies, he sees the man
with the red beard dressed in green;
on his chest he feels an icy hand,
hears a whisper cold and mean.

The next morning, the old man walked
down the lane in the fresh, clean air.
He saw two whitened bodies
that lay in the gutter there.

The fat innkeeper ran after him,
and gave him his gold entire;
for his name was sewn in the leather purse,
and they sang in the parish choir.

The old man went to the village church,
found a man to dig a grave,
and paid the priest to bury the boys,
and pray, their souls to save.

And, on their gravestone, he had carved
a pious, simple rhyme;
and then he went about his life,
and lived for the longest time.

Beowulf in Downtown D.C.

He walked, wild in wimpy wind,
past progressive piffle-poofs,
bearded briefcased bankers whose
soft steak-sated bellies bulged,
hairy hazy hoods whose thick
eyelids drooped with darkened dreams.
Asians and North-Africans,
blonds, browns and blacks, strutted boldly,
preening sidewalk monster meat.
Smart-phone slinging senoritas,
back-pack-bulging tourists with
mouths like cream of mushroom soup,
jostled in the urban jive.
Shiny bikes went whirring past
grimly jogging fitness fiends,
giant woofs on leather leash,
wag-tail weirdness, witless wool,
miniature mongrel mites,
flares of fur with torqued tails,
seeking schnauzer satisfaction:
flower beds in urban parks
where their sapient servants hurried
after them with humble haste.
Around him screamed falafel fiends,
flaunting fried peas soaked with sauce,
fairy feasts of drooling dough.
Weirdoes watched him from within
stealthy Starbucks darkened depths.
Even Beowulf could scarce
guess what fate might fly around
the granite corner: whether ghastly
baby-boomer grinning ghosts,

smearing thumbs on smart-phone screens,
or macho Mexicans in groups,
simmering under slicked-up hair,
toothing tasty taco treats…

Cheese

Poets have been mysteriously silent on the subject of cheese.
—*G.K. Chesterton*

Cheese, cheese, cheese, cheese,
from runny white to chunky blue,
cheese, cheese, cheese, cheese:
I'm in love with cheese, not you.

Cheese is better than people:
no lust, no intrigue, no self.
It yanks on the nose with its sensory pull.
Head for the cheese on the shelf.

Stinky people make everyone flee;
stinky cheese is a perfume to people like me.
Which form of life strives more sincerely to please—
routine-looking neighbors, or fermenting cheese?

Can you imagine the cheese sitting idle,
in a hundred varieties ripening there,
worshipped by crackers encircling the idol?—
Wine poured into a glass just adds fuel to the dare.

Fly off to Europe as soon as you may,
and order the cheese in a velvet café.
Forget about love, or your unwritten play.
Soon you'll see life an entirely new way.

Shrimp Sonnet

Like countless jewels in deepest ocean set,
pearly crustaceans creep along the sand.
Swept by Poseidon to the fisher's net,
they transubstantiate from sea to land.

Fresh prawns, fried in the Asian manner, turn
into thick, sugary dumplings as they sear,
and fly into to the mouth, where spices yearn
to prick the tongue. A crunch brings up the rear.

Thus, ancient flavors and sea conspire,
with Chardonnay, to set man's spirit free.
The Chinese mustard adds a tickling fire,
and a high richness fills the nose with glee.

Hail to thee, oh shrimp that feeds the man;
While others wilt in heat, you bang the pan.

Mediterranean Diet

I'm going on the Mediterranean Diet.
Shh—don't tell anyone. Please keep it quiet.
My mother, who was from an Italian family, made
meat loaf wrapped in bacon, and inlaid
with cornichons, and crumbs. She baked it in
tomato paste—a diet, and a sin.

Next comes the pasta—pour on the thick, white
bubbly cheese sauce, which is yours by right.
What? You demure? It won't help make you thin?
It may not help you lose; and yet, you'll win.
Here's why: each time I go to Italy,
trains whisk me past small farm plots by the sea:

outside the window, cows take in the air.
If milk weren't healthy, how could they be there?
If your cheese comes from Mediterranean cows
it has to satisfy your diet vows.
Transubstantiated into cheese,
Italian cow's milk will both cure, and please.

Once, in Bologna, I went to a fine
old restaurant, to try the food and wine.
I ordered broth with tortellini. They stuff it
with pork, and pour on parmesan to fluff it.
I gazed at it, then gazed across the white
linen-clad room and saw a novel sight.

In the far aisle, several old, and gray
waiters pushed a giant chrome steam tray.
The senior waiter, clearly high in rank,
grasped silver tongs and dipped into the tank,
reeling out something that looked quite a bit
like fire hose, and cut a length of it.

Two bearded diners gazed at the great cart,
eagerly waiting for the feast to start.
With a wrist-flick experienced and fey,
the waiter served them both, then rolled away.
"What are they being served?" I said to mine.
"Sir, those two gentlemen come here to dine

on a classic mix of ten meats, ground and creamed,
with twenty spices, stuffed in tripe, then steamed.
We've served it here since the 12th century.
Would you like to try some after the tortellini?"
I demurred, due to petty bourgeois fears.
But that shows health goes back 900 years.

As for the desert, I'll take the lemon cake
grounded on flour for the lemon's sake,
enriched with eggs from hens that breathe the air
of Mediterranean waters, cool and fair,
on plots of farmland where a few sheep gleep,
and wind in trees sends working men to sleep.

And what of the hot chocolate? Melt it, whole,
and pour it in a little silver bowl.
Ladle it freely on the lemon cake.
Then put gelato on the top to make
a healthy treat. Combine the frozen flavors,
with their savory fruits, their subtle savors,

to cool the chocolate as you ply your spoon:
avoiding excess heat in the afternoon
is one essence of an excellent day.
That's what Mediterranean people know, and say.

Protein Powder

You recommend a protein powder,
but I'd rather eat clam chowder.
White clam chowder's right for me:
sweet liquid sausage of the sea.

Go home to your Danish modern house;
and sanitize your Apple mouse:
then drink a protein powder shake;
and brush the gluten off the cake.

Lie on your latex bed with slats,
do yoga moves on fiber mats.
Whatever you do, perhaps it may
extend your life one single day.

Think of clam chowder oozing thick
from the rich depths that cling and stick,
with a fine alabaster gleam,
full of potato chunks, and cream.

I live where the wild things are,
close to an urban oyster bar.
I'll dine and clammy danger dare.
You may eat powder, water, air.

Frustrated Scholar

For 20 years I labored on
my life of Aneurin Bevan,
the first postmodern one, my pride,
and I was lost in Bevan heaven.
Even in the 7-11,
my every bite was Bevan leaven.
In my mind I lived the life
of the great Welsh laborer, his strife,
scratching coal on aching knees,
striking in gray factories,
in the Northlands, where fine men
fought for their rights, with speech and pen.
Unwilling to submit, or crawl,
self-educated, book by book,
he learned to stand and speak, and look,
and work for those who stoop and fall.
In my writing years, I travelled hard,
across the Atlantic many times—
and lost my wife to a British bard,
who published well, and fudged his rhymes;
but his example showed the way,
as we still struggle on today.
Just when the manuscript was done,
2,000 pages minus one,
Bob Micklemaus collapsed and died—
my editor and mental bride.
His boss at university press
first acted nice at my distress,
but said to cut the book in half.
I refused the golden calf—
and that triggered some contract clause
that meant he wasn't bound by laws.

Twenty years slipped up on grease,
and mankind lost a masterpiece.
I swear to God I thought the world
would reach out as my work unfurled
into the sky, a burning kite
to light the modern vulgar night,
his excellent biography
drawing the finest minds to me:
so gracious scholars everywhere
would come and breathe the country air
here in Vermont, where good things are,
trees, and bees, café and bar.
I'd kill myself, I swear to God,
but then I'd rot and turn to sod.
The lawyers think I have a case
and that they'll cave in to save face.
My new girlfriend is really sexy;
she saves me from an apoplexy.
It's too horrible to think.
I'll pop a Welsh craft beer, and drink.

Dictators Visit an Old Guy in the Maine Winter

Ere doe 'gan frolic in the springtime glade,
he knocked his fishing tackle off the shelf.
The hit lure slammed the floor, and then it made
a single bounce, like an insane, small elf.

The car was stallin' in the driveway too.
In fact, he didn't know quite what to do.
The cat had run someplace she shouldn't go;
he'd have to seize 'er in the winter snow.

He went to buy a funnel at the store.
Oh poo, tin funnels simply wouldn't do.
He'd buy aluminum for one buck more,
and then he'd pour the cooking oil through.

The freezing air cast a wintry pall.
Pot and kettle played their keening fife.
He trimmed some meat he'd bought down at the mall,
and sliced the bone apart, with his good knife.

He felt the little twinge within his knee.
Row and ride your bike, the doctor said.
He took a little sip of aging whisky—
sometimes, he felt it going to his head.

His neighbor had lawn problems, swear to God.
Come spring he'd bring his neighbor, Al, a sod.
He drove to see his girlfriend, Catherine.
The Great Dane barked at him as he came in.

The guy next to him in church had a loud voice.
Oh firk him, ill-sung hymns were worse than none.
Next time he'd try and make a better choice
of where to sit, so he could have some fun.

Beatified, he went down to the loo.
Eee. The 14th guy just got in line.
He'd have to wait for 14 minutes, too,
but after that, his bladder would be fine.

Ty, beerious, stumbled down the street.
He wasn't someone that he'd choose to meet,
and so he quickly crossed the other way.
Ty didn't even notice him—hooray.

Catherine had offered Sunday pie and tea.
Ty has nothing to pawn. Tea. Us. Pie. Late.
Golly, he'd loafed along since church got free.
He'd have to move his legs to make the date.

My Dog

My dog is a bundle of sweet, fuzzy love:
I love his hair, the beard on his pink face,

the way he hooks my leash to leather glove,
and lets me guide him, docile, place to place,

his squirrely armpit smell and sweaty socks,
and the two legged trot with which he rocks,

hoping to lure the female of his kind.
Sadly for him, the females are quite blind.

He looms above me, with each bush we pass,
and sometimes I confuse his head and ass,

as he bows, humble, to my nature's call.
Can anyone conceive a fault at all?

He lives for me. He shampoos the thick rug
I lie on all day—if I wish—a slug;

he even feeds me kibbles with his paw.
I really think the doggy is in awe

of my crouch stance, and tail-wagging grace.
I see the admiration in his face.

I hope that he'll soon mingle, mate, and breed
a whey-faced whelp to scratch my ass, in need.

Great Arf, who wags His tail in the sky,
gave me my dog to make the hours fly.

Sheep

They think that I'm a sweater, or roast meat—
the old man, and the boy, who drive our herd.
They think that I can't hear them, when I bleat,
but I perceive their speech, parse every word,

and can't reply. For it's an ancient plot.
A wizard spell stole all our speech away;
the human being got to where he got
with evil magic, on some ancient day.

They lust for our cheese spread, and our roast
slivered with garlic, spooned with curried fruit;
if I were king, I'd ban both cheese and toast,
and pull out garlic, to the bulb and root.

They talk and say that they are Socialists,
want to revolt against their higher kind.
Well, I'm a Socialist. I've made my lists;
and you're the first. The kid's not far behind.

This herd's complacent. But I feel bound,
too tight, in fleece and my four legs—I swear,
I'd like to butt them both, right off the ground,
but I'd be punished, so I do not dare.

In the next life, my friends, if we should meet,
I hope that I have sticks, and dogs worth fearing,
and you have hooves. Then you can stand and bleat,
and give milk. I'll make sheep jokes, during shearing.

Don't Read This Poem

Likely, this poem won't be very good.
Best not to waste your time on it; go out
and buff the wax around the pickup hood,
or see if you can find your neighbor lout

ridiculed on the Internet. Or shop
that Web site for a porcelain figurine.
Maybe it's time to make the popcorn pop,
and watch the series that your best friend's seen.

Should you want to read better than the spam,
go to the dusty shelf you used to use,
and drag out *In Memoriam*—
in those days, brains had a much longer fuse—

and undertake the Tennysonian slog.
If you read this, you'll turn into a frog.

Appendix: Key to the Dictators

Erdogan, Hitler, Stalin, Caesar, Putin, Pol Pot, Bonaparte, Nero, Al-Assad, Catherine the Great, Kim Il-Sung, Louis XIV, Tiberius, Pontius Pilate.

FINIS

About the Author

Paul Francis Malamud (b. 1947) has been writing, and translating, verse since his student days. Following college, a B.A. in British and French literature (1969), and a Ph.D. in British Literature (1980), he worked as a writer and editor for the U.S. government, in Washington, D.C.. He retired in 2008. His chapbook, *Horace and the French,* (Kelsay Books) contains verse translations from Latin and Renaissance French.